MW01439674

Unshackled

Precious Oshideko
Unshackled

All rights reserved
Copyright © 2023 by Precious Oshideko

No part of this publication may be reproduced, distributed, or transmitted in any form or by any means, including photocopying, recording, or other electronic or mechanical methods, without the prior written permission of the publisher, except in the case of brief quotations embodied in critical reviews and certain other noncommercial uses permitted by copyright law.
All scripture quotations are from the King James Version of the Bible unless otherwise indicated.

Published by BooxAi
ISBN: 978-965-578-860-0

Unshackled

Precious Oshideko

Introduction

In the day and age that we live in, so much is happening around us so fast we may sometimes feel like life has left us behind, and we are struggling to catch up—or conclude we can't and give up on trying. I wish you could hear me right now saying, "Get up! You're not done yet."

With this in mind, I have put together this collection of words in short stories and quotes, inspired by my life experience and interactions with people over the years, urging you to open your eyes and see that endless possibilities abound.

Success is different things to different people, so I do not assume we all want the same things in life. Whatever your definition of success may be, I hope that you will find within these pages the strength you need to force open the vast potential you have within you. Whether you need to let go of a painful past, learn to enjoy the gift of the present or reach out for a more meaningful future, give the words in this book a chance to change your thinking.

I do not claim to bring you any novel ideas, for in truth, there is nothing new under the sun. I only hope to light a fire in a heart

INTRODUCTION

already soaked in gasoline, to cause you to burn enough to say no to less and live your best life while it is yet morning.

It's a journey of faith for the courageous. The hand of God rests upon you. I see you winning. Amen.

— PRECIOUS

Lesson 1
Advice From a Janitor

I have been privileged to head some organizations in the last few years. Expectedly, time and again, I've been faced with making strategic decisions to ensure growth and attain set objectives. Some of these decisions have kept me up at night as I prayed and hoped things would work out as anticipated.

On one occasion, in a new country, working with new executives, we were faced with the issue of getting a new facility for our weekly operations.

My new team had suggestions that I considered needlessly grandiose, as no one could affirm the availability of any facility with the proposed features.

As our search intensified, I often got home completely exhausted after an all-day fruitless search and discussions with the executives and management. I had begun to feel a tinge of frustration because I didn't know the next step to take.

Very early one morning, I arrived at our office complex. Instead of going straight to my office, I went into the general office, where the janitors, cleaners, and office assistants converged. I sat with and engaged them in a light conversation about family, kids, and general everyday things. It was a heartwarming few minutes for me.

As I got up to leave, one of the janitors walked up to me, somewhat cautiously, and asked to speak with me privately. Of course, I obliged. I was curious.

He cleared his throat. "Sir," he began almost inaudibly, "I know we have been looking for a new facility, and there have been several suggestions."

I nodded in affirmation.

"There is a building not too far from the office that I think you should check out. Though a little run down, I'm confident we can renovate it with a few thousand dollars and turn it into a masterpiece."

He continued, "I've spoken to the owners, and they are willing to give it to us at almost nothing after the renovation."

Trying not to get my hopes up, I asked him to get in the car, and we drove to the facility.

I was amazed. What I saw was beauty hidden in dust and dilapidated walls and floors. It was a no-brainer. Our search was over.

The solution did not come from my most passionate, well-traveled management; it came from a humble janitor.

> *A great and strong wind rent the mountains, and brake in pieces the rocks before the Lord; but the Lord was not in the wind, and after the wind an earthquake; but the Lord was not in the earthquake: and after the earthquake a fire; but the Lord was not in the fire: and after the fire a still small voice (1 Kings 19: 11-12).*

Sometimes, we ignore the voice of wisdom around us because it is not dressed in an Italian suit and a red tie.

Lesson 2
Be Intentional

Plan it and do it.

Lesson 3
What Is Home for You?

Precious Oshideko

In the marketplace, we fight every day.

We fight to get to the top at work and fight to stay at the top. We fight to halt false accusers and fight to prove our worth.

There is a saying that everything looks like a nail to a man with a hammer. But home should be a place of peace and joy—refreshing for the battered soldier.

Strong man, don't confuse your home folks with the enemy outside. Before you head home from the marketplace, leave your sword behind.

Lesson 4
Step One

First of all, start.

Lesson 5
Wisdom for Men

Segun: Sir, I believe in this my line of business. It's my passion. I only need a sponsor or someone to help me with a good contact. I will use this business to shake the world.

PP: Segun, leave shaking the world alone for now. Find something to do to provide for your wife and children's basic needs, no matter how small.

Lesson 6
We Need One Another

Sometimes, because of all the battles of life, you are too tired to open the door: maybe the door of success, the door of a new job. You are so tired that all you have is strength enough to knock, and you need somebody from inside to open for you to come in.

Don't think you need no one—that is the thinking of fools. Be nice to people. You may one day need them to open the door.

Lesson 7
Not Too Late

Take that step. It's never too late.

Lesson 8
It's Not Permanent

Even though I walk through the valley of the shadow of death, I fear no evil (Psalm 23: 4).

We often face immense and intense pressure and want to give up. The psalmist says it's a shadow; it's not real. That means you are coming out of that situation.

When you are a Christian, there is a different life inside you—the life of God. The highest form of revelation is

> "Christ in me, the hope of glory" (Colossians 1:27).

This is more than "He is with me" or "He is protecting me."

He lives in you. That trouble will come to pass.

Lesson 9
Failure Not an Option

We don't stop. We push harder.

Lesson 10
Look in the Mirror, Sir

Frequently, we mistreat those weaker individuals around us, who may not have the ability to react or respond.

As a leader, it becomes challenging for people to inform you when you're making unwise decisions. Consequently, you might remain unaware of your mistakes for an extended period, as those around you constantly praise you and reinforce the belief that you are exceptional.

Sometimes, it's crucial to take a step back and engage in introspection. Ask yourself: Am I a good person? Am I kind to others?

In the silence of a sincere heart, the answers will emerge.

Lesson 11
Fine Boy

Don't let your desire to project a "fine boy" image take priority over your legitimate, everyday hustle. If you end up a broke "fine boy", even your family will despise you.

Lesson 12
Do Butterflies Still Make You Smile?

After several years of fighting many battles—maybe losing a loved one, being betrayed by friends, making sacrifices for family, losing a job, going through a divorce or separation—we become like vicious warriors, our perception of the world so altered as a result of pain and disappointments, it becomes difficult to trust again without reservation, and we lose our beautiful nature-given, gentle spirit.

As you read this chapter, be encouraged to look within and find that beautiful you again. Do not, for fear of disappointment, be afraid to love and trust again. Your heart is big enough to handle it.

Lesson 13
Nothing Wasted

Ensure you seize the lessons that failure offers.

Lesson 14
Glass Houses

He that is without sin among you, let him first cast a stone at her (John 8:7).

Jesus' words reminded the self-righteous men ready to stone a woman to death that they were no better than her.

The Bible says they all felt convicted and

"went out one by one, beginning at the eldest, even unto the last" (John 8:9).

Empathy is important. Put yourself in others' shoes before picking up that stone.

Lesson 15
Never Too Late

At twenty-three, you cannot complain your parents did not send you to school. Send yourself to school.

At forty-five, don't say, "Time has gone; I am too old to learn a new skill."

No! Don't believe that lie. You're not too old; you've still got time.

Lesson 16
Grace to Flourish

When grace goes with you, everything you touch will flourish.

LESSON 17
VOICES IN MY HEAD

Their voices were in my head.
The things they said I couldn't do.
I was hearing them inside my head,
but I had my own voice telling me, "You can do it!"
So, I cut them off, that my inner voice could rise because I needed my voice to fight.
Then, my voice increased inside me.
And then, I was able to conquer my own battles.

Lesson 18
You Are Your Own Priority

Quit keeping scores on how many people were not there to help you when you needed them. How many were you there to help when they needed you?

Move on. Life is beautiful. Enjoy it.

Lesson 19
A Note to My Child

Listen, my child.

I will tell you of two ways money comes to a person:

1. Money comes through favours from other people. They can give you money if they like or consider you relevant to them. I've seen this happen many times.

2. Money also comes through acquiring skills that create solutions to people's needs. If you get this right, people will look for you anytime and anywhere in the world to give you money in exchange for your services.

Of these two ways, my child, you only have control over one.

For the day your benefactors no longer like you, or you do or say something they don't like, they could withdraw their favours and make others they influence do the same; thus, you can go from a hundred to zero in one day.

Ohun ti a ba fara sise fun, Nii pe lowo eni.

[It is what we genuinely work for that lasts.]

Choose wisely.

Lesson 20
Don't Be Deceived

Your mind will tell you you are too old to take the challenge. Don't listen.

Lesson 21
Thanks, But Don't Give Me Fish

Friends often inquire why I didn't seek their financial assistance during my period of economic hardship. However, I never perceived the issue as merely a lack of money, despite facing financial constraints. The true challenge lay in the absence of skills to generate income. I lacked the essential marketplace skills for transactions, budgeting, savings, and investments—that was the core issue.

It's truly remarkable how acquiring the right skills can transform one's life.

LESSON 22
SMELL THE COFFEE

Stop deluding yourself, expecting a windfall. Take action—seek employment or acquire a new skill.

Lesson 23
Think Possible

Precious Oshideko

In my first week in class for a program I had enrolled in, I was dismayed to hear answers tumbling out of the mouths of my younger coursemates, even before I could understand any question the lecturer asked.

Completely distraught, I concluded my brain was not functioning like it should. *How come they all know the answers and I don't?*

One night, as I lay on the couch in my living room, feeling sorry for myself, all kinds of thoughts went through my mind: *Maybe this course isn't for me. Maybe my brain has reverted to a little child's brain, so much so I can no longer grab concepts.*

Then I remembered that crèches had *"A for apple"* splashed in bright colours on the walls and the board so that the children's brains could catch it. I decided to do the same.

The following day, I got large posters, pasted them on my study wall, and wrote out in bold lettering those concepts and definitions I struggled with and highlighted them in different bright colours. Then I sat down, night after night, looking at them, studying them.

By the following week, I was giving the class tutorials. My brain had come alive.

> "Once you stop learning, you start dying."
>
> — Albert Einstein

Lesson 24
Renew Your Thinking

You can still embrace a youthful mindset and become a person with innovative thinking, regardless of your age.

Lesson 25
Values

Success and achievements are a threat to the core values of any organization or individual. These two factors tempt us to think the value system that brought us to our current platform is no longer needed. We have seen in society how organizations that supposedly had sound values in the past lose those values as the organizations grow bigger.

It takes a great deal of effort by the leadership of any organization to continually insist on a re-appraisal of the core values, regeneration of the decaying ones, and reinventing ways of communicating these values effectively to employees.

For this reason, I agree with the statement, 'The only thing more dangerous than failure is success."

Too easily, we allow success to change our personality, robbing us of our fundamental ethics, principles, and core values.

Lesson 26
Table Manners

If you meet a successful and influential person, do not ask for money or favours, and don't talk about your problems. Let the friendship grow by engaging in intelligent conversations. Learn from them. You will be amazed at the opportunities they could guide you into.

Lesson 27
Project Yourself

Sing your own praise. Project your business.

If you don't preach yourself, nobody will preach you.

Lesson 28
The River Beckons

Unshackled

My dad told me many years ago, "Precious, it's not when you are thirsty you go to the river. You fetch water before you are thirsty."

I failed Physics but passed the subjects I needed for admission into the University.

In my second year, I told my friends, "I want to rewrite Physics."

"What do you need it for? You are already in the University," they said.

But I remembered my dad's words: "It's not when you are thirsty you go to the river."

When I graduated from the University, I got a good job. After a few months on the job, I told my friends, "Let's go do our master's."

"What do we need it for? We already have good jobs," they said.

But I remembered my dad's words.

Plan for tomorrow, today.

Lesson 29
Other People's Plates

I do not look at people and wish what they have is mine; neither do their achievements make me feel like I am behind in life.

Food loses its taste with our eyes constantly on other people's plates.

Lesson 30
Don't Go Down Easy

There is an account in the bible of a certain man named Abner, who was fighting against David, the King of Judah, for the house of Saul to reign over all the kingdom of Israel.

Eventually, circumstances caused Abner to seek David out for a peaceful reconciliation.

Now, this happened in the absence of David's chief of staff, Joab, who hated Abner because, during a previous battle, Abner had killed his younger brother.

When Joab returned to find out that Abner had come to town and left unharmed, he sent messengers to bring him back. Deceiving him into thinking he wanted to speak with him privately, he took him aside and stabbed him to death.

When David heard that Joab had killed Abner, he unleashed a tirade of curses at Joab and his household. Then, weeping at the grave of Abner, he said something profound:

> *And the king lamented over Abner and said, Died Abner as a fool dieth? Thy hands were not bound, nor thy feet put into fetters (2 Samuel 3:33 - 34).*

I get fired up every time I read those words. And whenever a situation tries to cause me to bow, I tell myself, "Precious, don't go down like a fool."

Never let your mind or society deceive you into thinking you are tied down to your present, unfavourable circumstance. If opportunity doesn't come for you, go for it!

Lesson 31
What Do You Have In Your Hands?

Don't be fixated on another's money, hoping to get something for nothing. What service can you offer?

Lesson 32
Everyone Needs an Eraser

Writing has always been a hobby for me. I love to scribble down my thoughts and basic perceptions of life.

Lately, I find myself sketching faces, trees, and anything that catches my attention.

Recently, while about this nascent hobby, I sketched a man's face but was displeased with the outcome because it didn't look happy. So, I took my eraser, cleaned out the bold facial lines, and made it lighter. Then I adjusted the cheekbones a little—and voila!—my amateur drawing was smiling at me. I smiled back, pleased.

We must learn the power of the eraser—how to let go, shut a door and leave it closed, and how to draw another line in our artwork.

Life is a journey. Enjoy the twists and turns, but start all over if you have to, fearing nothing.

I love the story of Isaac in the Bible. A man with an unstoppable spirit:

> *And he removed from thence, and digged another well (Genesis 26:22).*

How beautiful it is to have the courage to let go, move forward, and dig again.

Lesson 33
What Matters Most?

Prioritise and value family. Maintain close ties with great friends close; genuine connection with good people are rare.

Lesson 34
Fantasies

Classy and beautiful. Smooth and compact. The colour blended with the reflection of the morning sun.

Staring in admiration, I wished I was the one behind the wheels.

"It is the latest model," my friend whispered.

I took my phone to google the features of this beauty before me. "This is amazing," I muttered, beholding the latest technology in this ultimate ride—this Machine.

My fingers were pinned on Google search over the next few days as I watched, again and again, videos displaying the features of this vehicle on YouTube and even more videos comparing it to other cars of the same year.

I wished I had them all—the four-wheel-drive truck for my construction work, farm work, and the unpaved road in my terrain; the sedan for a gentle drive on a lazy Sunday evening; the wagon for trips to neighbouring states and long drives, and the convertible for picnics and parties with friends.

Then came a strong, compelling voice from within, jolting me back to reality: "These fantasies will soon make you steal if you are not careful."

Making money is an art to be studied, practised, and perfected. It is a skill that can deliver your future right into your hands. Step out of the realm of fantasy and acquire the skill you need.

Lesson 35
Can We Just Talk?

If every conversation with you is tied around the difficulties you are facing, you'll make friendship difficult.

Lesson 36
Unshackled

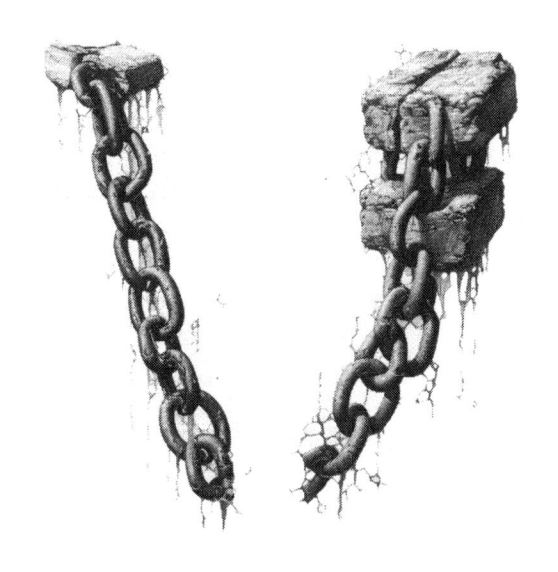

I've discovered that I don't need others to believe in my capabilities;
I've liberated myself from the need for human validation.

Lesson 37
Receive Instruction

I am fascinated by Proverbs 24: 30-32.

I went by the field of the slothful, and by the vineyard of the man void of understanding; and, lo, it was all grown over with thorns, and nettles had covered the face thereof, and the stone wall thereof was broken down. Then I saw, and considered it well: I looked upon it, and received instruction.

It matters how you see.

The writer was taking a stroll by the vineyard of a lazy man and saw how disorganized things were. He said, *"I looked upon it and received instruction."* What instruction? Perhaps he heard a voice telling him never to let his life or vineyard take this pattern.

What voice do you hear as you observe a friend's business fold up? — As a friend narrates how he got rejected at an interview? As people sit down and complain about the economy of nations?

You must train yourself to see a brighter day anytime doubt tries to becloud your thoughts. Also, if you happen to stroll by the vineyard of a wise man, stop, look upon it, and receive instruction and strategy for yours.

Lesson 38
Stoke the Fire

The fire is in the mind. So what happens when the fire goes out?
What happens when you don't know how to restart the fire?

Lesson 39
Glitters

I always get compliments about my house. However, the journey from foundation to completion took ten years. During that time, sometimes, I felt motivated to keep building; other times, I felt like giving up and selling off. There were periods when all the money I had could only get forty blocks of cement—or just a few irons—or nothing.

Through all this, my principle was, "Every step forward is success, no matter how short the step."

Social media can give the impression of instant wealth. But in reality, getting results in life is not magic. It's consistency. It's patience.

Other builders around me started and finished their houses within three to six months. I couldn't. It was not a competition. I was content to run my marathon step-by-step.

Don't lose courage as you build your life: your relationships, your business, or even your house. Be proud of your journey. Be consistent.

> *For precept must be upon precept, precept upon precept; line upon line, line upon line; here a little, and there a little (Isaiah 28:10).*

Lesson 40
You Decide

Change your circle, shift your mindset, and you possess the power to transform any aspect of yourself. The choice is yours.

Lesson 41
Make It Work

Things don't work out for you because you are a good person; things work out for you because you have planned intentionally.

Lesson 42
The Music Inside

Often, we desire to dance, yet we wait for someone else to provide the music. I propose the music is within you; just let it play, and dance.

Lesson 43
How Much Are You Worth?

Currency is not only in money; it is also in relationships. Don't make your world too small. Open yourself to people. Open yourself to opportunities.

Lesson 44
The Words in Silence

Getting home exhausted after a busy day at work, I hit the couch, hoping to catch a short nap before completing a few tasks.

Within a few minutes, I was asleep.

Too soon, I was recalled from my trip by his little fingers poking my mouth, eyes, and ears.

I tried to get my two-year-old son's hand off me so I could nap a little longer. He kept poking and muttering some baby talk I was unprepared to give attention to.

The battle continued for about three minutes before I finally decided to carefully listen to the sounds he was muttering while still keeping my eyes closed, unwilling to give up my sleep mission.

Suddenly, I figured he was saying "mouth, ears, eyes" as he touched my face. He was practising what he learned at the crèche!

I opened my eyes with a smile. Instantly, there was a paradigm shift. What I thought was a great disturbance turned out to be the most beautiful words in my ears when I decided to be patient and give it attention.

Sometimes, all we need is to calm down and listen.

Lesson 45
Recognize Your Limits

One of the quickest paths to being broke is attempting to be kind to everyone. Acknowledge your limitations and avoid stretching yourself too thin.

Lesson 46
Say No to Pressure

If you happen to drop something, simply bend down, pick it up, and carry on. There's no shame in pausing and giving yourself the chance to begin anew.

Lesson 47
Does He Speak Portuguese?

It was a beautiful summer evening on the Lehigh University campus. Race, sex, and religion were no barriers. Twelve of us came from different countries and backgrounds, with varying outlooks to life. Among us were PhD holders, medical professionals, academics, engineers, photographers, etc.

Under the silent, friendly gaze of the full moon, we all sat, forming a circle on the well-mowed lawn, like children in a bonding time with their parents.

As we discussed different cultures and national issues, I brought up the subject of the love of God, His forgiveness, and the Cross; a topic I had to introduce in the friendliest and most relaxed manner, careful not to invite unnecessary antagonism, dispute, or any other negative response.

They all listened with rapt attention as I spoke calmly. It was a beautiful moment. We had no care for time, the world, or anything; we were utterly enraptured in God's love.

Then I announced that I wanted us to pray—to pour out our hearts to the one who hears our prayers and discusses them with no other.

Everyone prayed fervently.

After a few minutes, I opened my eyes to see one of my friends not praying. She looked lost. I moved close to her and whispered in her ears, "Why aren't you praying?"

"Precious," she said, "I don't speak English fluently. I cannot pour out my heart in English."

And with the innocence of a child, she asked, "Does Jesus speak Portuguese?"

Oh, how that warmed my heart.

"Yes, He does," I assured her. "He speaks all languages!"

Immediately, she bowed her head and began to pray in the language she was most fluent in. Tears flowed freely from her eyes as she poured her heart out to Jesus Christ our Lord.

Lesson 48
Plan, Plan, Plan

That organization doesn't belong to you. Your desk in the office today will be someone else's tomorrow. One era ends, and another begins. Plan for the future intentionally, for it is on the horizon.

Lesson 49
The Voice of a Seven-Year-Old

As I approached the entrance of the audition venue, I was welcomed by a group of excited young people from different counties in Dallas, Texas, anxious to perform and get my assessment after several weeks of intense training.

Everyone prayed to get a good score at this stage of the auditions and qualify for an appearance at the big event.

I watched several presentations and gave my analysis and commendation after each performance.

The best artists received a loud ovation from the audience, and my commendations elicited even more applause.

Amidst all the excitement, I learned one of the greatest lessons of my life.

A group of five teenage boys had given an exceptional performance, and I intended to approve the presentation and give the group a ticket to perform at the upcoming event. However, I had a problem with the lead singer. He was not as lively as the backup singers and dancers but appeared laid back and shy.

Addressing the young man, I said, "I like your song, but you need to sing more like a man and not act weak."

"Thank you, sir," he quietly responded.

The audience applauded the group as they left the stage.

At that moment, a little girl, about seven years old, walked up to my table and stood beside me. She probably came with her elder brother or sister to watcShe said, "I think you should have just told the boy to put more energy into his song instead of telling him to sing like a man. When you leave, everyone will laugh at him that he sings like a girl, and he will go home unhappy."

She said, "I think you should have just told the boy to put more energy into his song instead of telling him to sing like a man. When you leave, everyone will laugh at him that he sings like a girl, and he will go home unhappy."

I sincerely never thought of that. I didn't consider the impact my comment could have on the young man following the audition.

I learned wisdom from a seven-year-old.

This experience has influenced my communication. Now, before I speak, I consider what I am about to say and the impact it could have on the life of the person I am addressing.

We learn every day. Never get to a point in life where you are too big to learn from younger people around you or too mighty to see the wisdom in an employee's sincere suggestion.

I pray that God will use things, objects, events, and people around you to speak to and teach you so you can be ready for the great heights ahead.

Lesson 50
Keep Moving

At times, your forecasts may not align with reality. That's completely normal; persevere. You might believe you aced an interview, only to face rejection. It's inconsequential. Keep pushing forward. As long as you breathe, keep moving.

Lesson 51
Masqueraders

I engaged in a conversation with a woman who professed her belief in prosperity through the word of God. She passionately shared how she fervently prays for anyone discontented with her business success to face misfortune or lose something significant.

I questioned, 'What is the worth of your business that it warrants wishing harm upon someone merely for being dissatisfied with it?'

Regrettably, some fail to grasp the fundamental principles of Christianity. They hold the bible but have a *babalawo's* mindset.

Lesson 52
Consider the Ant

You suddenly discover the push is gone at a certain stage in your life. You are no longer interested in the things that used to drive the younger you: money, the desire to improve yourself or learn new skills. All you want now is a life of quiet— eat, watch TV, and relax with close friends.

That period happens to all, and we often don't even see it coming. The danger is that people do not use the period of passion and strength to save, invest, and plan for this phase of life's journey.

Winter is coming, my friend; prepare ahead.

Lesson 53
Let Wisdom Direct You

I talked with a young man named Michael, who had dropped out of school. I tried to convince him to go back to school.

He said, "I'm twenty-five now. It will be four years before I'm done with school. I'll be twenty-nine. I'll be too old."

I told him, "But if you don't go to school, you will still be twenty-nine in four years."

Lesson 54
Face It Then Change It

When you find yourself in a low point, acknowledge it, and without shame, engage in actions that will lift you back up.

BLURB

"I don't profess to introduce groundbreaking concepts, for in truth, there is nothing entirely new under the sun. My sole aim is to kindle a flame within a heart already soaked in gasoline, compelling you to burn brightly enough to reject mediocrity and embrace your optimal life while the day is still young."

— PRECIOUS OSHIDEKO

In "Unshackled," Precious Oshideko skillfully employs quotes and short stories to deliver transformative messages that prompt a reassessment of your thoughts, lifestyle, and aspirations.

Feeling overwhelmed by life's journey?

Exhausted from the effort?

Believing it's too late?

Uncertain where to begin?

This enjoyable, one-sitting read, with its nuanced yet direct approach, encompasses wisdom derived from the author's life experiences and years of coaching and mentoring individuals and groups. It will inspire you to liberate yourself from self-imposed limitations, conquer defeat, and embrace the greatness rightfully yours.

About the Author

Precious Oshideko is the founder of Arete-Zale Consulting, a free global training platform that

equips young people to explore modern work opportunities and connects them with practical

resources for harnessing their full potential. Propelled by an affinity for youth and development, he

has organized and spoken at Youth conferences in over 100 higher institutions in Africa, United States and Asia. He is currently steering the strategic role of Vice President in a Fortune 100 company. Nonetheless, his influence extends beyond the boardroom to online thought leadership with content curated to help his followers build intellectual capacity, develop social-emotional dexterity and explore relevant opportunities.

He is popularly known for his Not Too Old conferences, where he inspires participants to pick up

their boots and keep running.

Precious lives in Dallas, Texas, with his family.

Connect with Precious:
Website: www.aretezale.com

facebook.com/DavidPreciousOshideko
instagram.com/presh_osh

Made in the USA
Columbia, SC
02 March 2024

513d64cd-9309-452d-9122-042ee7a05ed8R01